LICE
Head Hunters

BARBARA A. SOMERVILL

PowerKiDS press™

New York

Published in 2008 by The Rosen Publishing Group, Inc.
29 East 21st Street, New York, NY 10010

First Edition

Editor: Joanne Randolph
Book Design: Dean Galiano
Layout Design: Greg Tucker
Photo Researcher: Nicole Pristash

Photo Credits: Cover, p. 21 © David Scharf/Getty Images; pp. 5, 11, 15, 17 © Shutterstock.com; pp. 7, 9, 13 by James Gathany/CDC/Frank Collins, Ph.D.; p. 19 by Janice Carr/CDC/Joseph Strycharz, Ph.D., Kyong Sup Yoon, Ph.D., Frank Collins, Ph.D.

Library of Congress Cataloging-in-Publication Data

Somervill, Barbara A.
   Lice : head hunters / Barbara A. Somervill. — 1st ed.
      p. cm. — (Bloodsuckers)
   Includes index.
   ISBN-13: 978-1-4042-3803-9 (library binding)
   ISBN-10: 1-4042-3803-4 (library binding)
   1. Pediculosis—Juvenile literature. 2. Lice—Juvenile literature. I. Title.
   RL764.P4S66 2008
   616.5'72—dc22
                                                2006103424

Manufactured in the United States of America

CONTENTS

MEET THE LOUSE

A note comes home from school, and Mom makes a horrible face. The school is warning adults to check their children for head lice. Head lice are a common problem in schools.

If you do have lice, now begins the hard part. For days, you will need to wash your hair with lice-killing shampoo and comb your hair with a fine-tooth comb. Head lice do not go away unless all the eggs, called nits, are removed.

There are ways to help stop the spread of lice. Do not share things that you put on your head, such as brushes and hats.

5

LOTS OF LICE

There are between 5,500 and 6,000 known **species** of lice around the world. They are broken into two groups. The first group is the chewing or biting lice, which is made up of more than 5,000 species. They feed on the feathers of birds or the hide of cattle or sheep. They do not drink blood.

Sucking lice are bloodsuckers. There are fewer than 500 species of sucking lice. They feed mostly on **mammals**. Unlike some **insects** that will feed on any mammal, different species of lice will feed on only certain kinds of animals.

This body louse is feeding on a person. Body lice are found in bedding, on clothing, and on people's bodies.

7

LOUSE LOOKS

A louse is a small, wingless insect that cannot fly or jump. It has a small, flat head with tiny eyes. Its body is flat, too.

Biting or chewing lice have **mandibles**. Sucking lice have narrow tubes in their mouth, called **stylets**. Biting lice tend to have a large head, while sucking lice have a thinner, smaller head. Both have a tiny, grayish body and short, stubby **antennae**. Although females are larger than males, most lice measure between ⅟₁₆ and ⅙ inch (1.6–4.2 mm).

This body louse has six legs and two antennae. The dark part on the body is blood that the louse ate before.

9

PICKY EATERS

A louse's **prey** is called a host. A louse does not munch on just any host, though. Whether the louse is a biting or sucking louse, it feeds mostly on one species of animal. One species of lice preys on elephants. Another species preys on warthogs. Chickens have several species of lice, such as body lice, head lice, wing lice, and shaft, or feather, lice.

Even fish can have lice. Lice cause **itching**, and hosts peck, rub, and roll in mud to stop it.

Even sea animals struggle with lice. Lice live on seals and sea lions just as they live on dogs and cats.

TIME FOR DINNER

Chewing or biting lice do not feed on blood meals. They use their sharp mandibles to gnaw away at their food. Some feed on feathers. Others eat hair or pieces of skin.

Sucking lice feed on blood as both **nymphs** and adults. The louse's stylet pokes through the host's skin. Then the louse sucks out a small amount of blood. Sucking lice cannot live away from their hosts. Without a blood meal, a louse will die. Lice cannot live over two days without feeding.

This sucking louse has poked its stylet through a person's skin. People may get small, red bumps on their skin from lice bites.

ONE-STOP SHOPPER

Lice are not hunters. Most often, they are born on their food supply and begin eating as soon as possible. The host is all things to a louse. It gives the louse a home, heat, and food.

Lice do not plan to move from one host to another. Among herd animals, such as cows and zebras, one lice-**infested** animal rubs against another. The eggs are then passed on to another animal. Among humans, lice may pass from one person to another when people's bodies touch.

Lice may become stuck in hats, combs, and brushes and move from person to person by sharing.

15

TASTY LICE

Wild animals cannot take a shower or wash with a lice-killing cleaner. They have found other ways to rid themselves of lice. Baboons and monkeys groom each other. When they groom, they pick lice and other insects from a friend's fur and eat them.

Water buffalo, giraffes, and elephants need help from birds like oxpeckers. These birds search their large mammal pals for lice, feeding on hundreds of insects in a day.

For sea animals that have lice, there are cleaner fish. Cleaners move around the animal's body, find the lice, and pluck them off for a meal.

The monkey on the right is grooming its friend. Monkeys spend part of each day cleaning each other's fur.

17

PEOPLE AND LICE

Three types of lice have an effect on people. They are head lice, body lice, and crab lice. Head lice are mostly found on children between the ages of 3 and 11. At those ages, children come in close **contact** with each other. The lice attack the neck, behind the ears, and the crown of the head.

Body lice are generally found in places where people must live close together and cannot wash often. Crab lice get their name because they look like tiny crabs. These lice are generally found only on adults.

This is a close-up picture of a body louse. In the United States, body lice are mainly found on people who cannot shower or wash their clothes often.

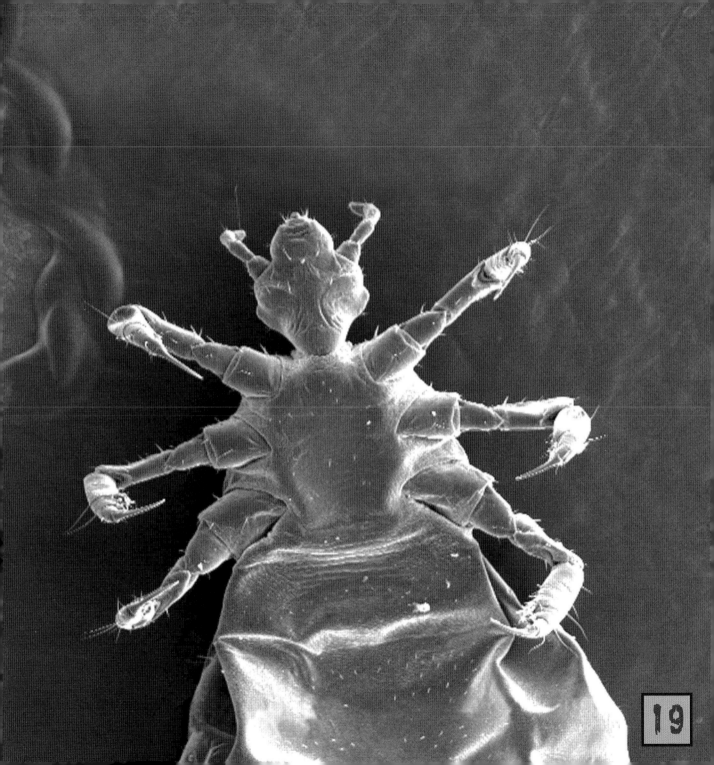

THE LIFE OF A LOUSE

All lice go through three body forms, which are egg, nymph, and adult. This is called a three-step **metamorphosis**. A female louse lays eggs. The number of eggs is different for different types of lice. The eggs are sticky and become glued to hair or clothing. They break open in 8 to 10 days.

The next life stage is the nymph stage. Nymphs look and act like tiny adult lice. They feed on blood and grow into adults in one week.

Adult lice drink blood and mate so they can produce more lice. Adults live about 35 to 40 days.

This is a close-up photo of a louse and an egg, called a nit. Body lice lay 275 to 300 nits, while head lice lay only 50 to 100 nits.

CONTROLLING LICE

If people or pets get lice, they may need help to get rid of them. Doctors and nurses can help a person deal with human lice. A **veterinarian** knows how to control animal lice.

A person with lice needs to shower and wash his or her hair daily, using lice-killing shampoo. Most drugstores sell creams, lotions, soaps, and shampoos made to rid the body of lice. A person with lice should also wash his or her bedding and clothes often. Although neither people nor animals can die from having lice, they can have skin problems from many bites.

GLOSSARY

antennae (an-TEH-nee) Thin, rodlike feelers on the head of certain animals.

contact (KON-takt) The touching or meeting of people or things.

infested (in-FEST-ed) Filled a place in a troublesome way.

insects (IN-sekts) Small animals that often have six legs and wings.

itching (ih-CHING) An uneasy feeling on the skin.

mammals (MA-mulz) Warm-blooded animals that have a backbone and hair, breathe air, and feed milk to their young.

mandibles (MAN-dih-bulz) The paired jaws of an insect that generally move side to side.

metamorphosis (meh-tuh-MOR-fuh-sus) A complete change in form.

nymphs (NIMFS) Young insects that have not yet grown into adults.

prey (PRAY) An animal that is hunted by another animal for food.

species (SPEE-sheez) One kind of living thing.

stylets (STY-lets) Pointy mouthparts made for cutting and for sucking juices.

veterinarian (veh-tuh-ruh-NER-ee-un) A doctor who treats animals.

INDEX

WEB SITES

Due to the changing nature of Internet links, PowerKids Press has developed an online list of Web sites related to the subject of this book. This site is updated regularly. Please use this link to access the list:
www.powerkidslinks.com/bsu/lice/